Praise for *Singing Me Home*

"The vibrant, memorable images that thread through Carol Lipszyc's moving collection would in themselves be enough to make *Singing Me Home* worth reading and re-reading: her depiction of a nun in a telephone booth as 'an angel on sabbatical,' of the booth's telephone directory as an 'Urban Book of Genesis,' or of the moon as 'a silver coin in the palm of night'—these images do what all good poetry should, freshening our experience of the world by polishing both its details and our vision. Yet, *Singing Me Home* offers much more. Infused with the awareness that the resources of poetry are 'poor intermediaries' between us and an often hostile and indecipherable world, Lipszyc's poems nevertheless use those resources—what else do we have?—to come to terms with the deepest mysteries of life, both its appalling tragedies (fire, personal loss, the unfathomable horrors of the Shoah) and its sudden, almost-redemptive joys (moments of harmony with nature, with others, with the self). Like the hum of the dashboard heater in her father's red Pontiac, singing her home from Hebrew School, Lipszyc's poems sing us home, to the heart of our shared humanity."
—JOHN REIBETANZ, award-winning poet and critic

"*Singing Me Home*, Carol Lipszyc's a compelling debut collection of poetry, is far more than a simple melody. The poems are filled with arresting images, metaphors, and turns of language. 'Reading Braille' is an example of brilliant, breathtaking, daring use of line length and stanza breaks. Careful and casual readers will both find pleasure in reading Lipszyc's *Singing Me Home*, which exemplifies well-crafted poems of keen observation and deep feeling."
—MIRIAM KOTZIN, author of *Reclaiming the Dead, Weights and Measures* and the upcoming, *Taking Stock*

"Carol Lipszyc's *Singing Me Home* is a hymn of praise to memory, to witness, and to those mysterious elements of the past, both individual and collective, that live on inside us. Alternately solemn and playful, mournful and joyous, it speaks clearly and eloquently to the deepest wells of our own ever-strange, ever-wondrous lives."
—MARK FREEMAN, author of *Hindsight: The Promise and Peril of Looking Backward* and *Rewriting the Self: History, Memory, Narrative*

Singing Me Home

poems by Carol Lipszyc

Inanna Poetry & Fiction Series

INANNA Publications and Education Inc.
Toronto, Canada

Canada Council **Conseil des Arts**
for the Arts du Canada

 ONTARIO ARTS COUNCIL
CONSEIL DES ARTS DE L'ONTARIO

The publisher gratefully acknowledges the support of the Canada Council for the Arts and the Ontario Arts Council for its publishing program.

The publisher is also grateful for the kind support received from an Anonymous Fund at The Calgary Foundation.

Cover design: Val Fullard
Cover artwork: Fiona H. Shields, untitled, 1992, pastel on board, 18" x 24".
Interior design: Luciana Ricciutelli

Library and Archives Canada Cataloguing in Publication

Lipszyc, Carol
      Singing me home : poems / by Carol Lipszyc.

(Inanna poetry and fiction series)
ISBN 978-1-926708-15-7

     I. Title. II. Series: Inanna poetry and fiction series

PS8623.I57S56 2010   C811'.6   C2010-906462-3

Printed and bound in Canada

Inanna Publications and Education Inc.
210 Founders College, York University
4700 Keele Street, Toronto, Ontario M3J 1P3 Canada
Telephone: (416) 736-5356 Fax (416) 736-5765
Email: inanna@yorku.ca Website: www.yorku.ca/inanna

for my mother, Rose

Contents

III

I.

Preserving Childhood

Ice-blue crinoline
behind stage curtains.

Workdays,
tub-white acrylic stains my father's face.
His flannel chest
is a pillow,
concave and soft.

From the freshly-waxed kitchen, five
bowls of vanilla pudding,
peaks of tart raspberry, cool
on my mother's mathematical counter.

Through vacant halls
a shrill bell ricochets,
slicing the day into quarters and halves.
Doors swing open
to a marathon of pent-up children
who stride, jump out of classrooms
and pummel the steep grey stairs.

In minutes, the schoolyard drums a feral beat

of rival cliques and rhyming chants,
and nebulous games of hide-and-seek.

Stairway curves to the warped cellar floor
where a black-speckled fountain spouts
water in a radius of expectation -
a summer shower on petal-shaped palms.

At the foot of the gravel driveway,
a garland in plastic purple —

whirring waist and swerving hip
I *hula-hoop*
with Dina to seal
a girlhood pact and press

time down, heart-shaped
and iridescent like leaves
before they scatter
in the lapses of wind.

Hebrew School

I

We chase pin-point dots
up, down and around
the topography of black, square script.

"Follow the *Ni-kku-dot*,[1] children,
marry vowels to the consonants,
and sound the words out...."

Teacher stirs in rote rhythm,
clink of metal spoon
in a porcelain cup of steam hot milk:

"*Alef, Beit, Gimel, Dalet....*"[2]

Marvin sustains the Hebraic 'h',
his gremlin hand clutching his throat.

"There's a fish bone lodged in Marvin's pharnyx!"

Oh, Hebrew script running backwards —
we are a dispersed tribe
testing our agility.

II

Ark doors front our temple.
Their weighty inscription,
Shaarei Shomayim,
reads:

Open heaven.

Still we clamor till dusk
in the shrill discontinuity of a generation.

III

Basement gymnasium: our black-caped leader
opens a sacred chest, lifts the Torah
scrolls, velvet cloak in ruby red, two
chambers of mystical molecule
words in quill pen ink.

Shema Israel[3] — insignia of
blue thread drapes the *bimah.*[4]

We bow our heads to sages and offer
scant Benediction: logan
berry juice in paper-cups
and white dough cookies sprinkled
in candy green and yellow.

Brother Alan,
in plaid jacket and bow tie,
counts blocks
all the way home,
dreams of black saucer
hockey pucks torpedoing
over ice, and the sirens
of fire trucks he can chase
as a brave cub at heart.

IV

Thursday evening,
gold-braided egg bread, *Challah*,
for the Sabbath bride.

Stretch a strand of yeast
to see how wide God's honey-laced
blessings can spread.

Our hunger noise quieted,
Mrs. Wise locks the classroom door,
and sits, elbows crossed
at her desk,
her gray, stiff hair,
a pylon

to tell how she once lived

in a bone yard
where ovens baked not bread
but people,
where chimneys spewed ashes —
and what did we think of that,
boys and girls?

Cave rock
in my belly, my chest.

I turn to Pnina,
whose parents own Herme's Bakery.
She might understand.

She stares into limbo —
the one
reserved for children
who carry sin
like unwashed fruit in a basket.

Marvin recoils, his face
hit by a blank bullet.

V

In his study
after class,
Rabbi Gordon launches a vessel
of questions,

and I am his disciple.

Chad Gadya[5]
One little goat for the father God
from of a flock of wanderers.

I sing tremolo
as the Rabbi taps
a rapid heartstring
of the story.

His voice,
the ebb of a fire
that burns the stick
that beats the dog that bites the cat.

Chaya, he says in Hebrew,
life endures in your name.

VI

Pillars loom
colossus.

Streetlights of St. Clair Avenue
blind me.

I leap into
Father's lone, red Pontiac,

the hum of the dashboard heater

singing me home.

[1] System of points that are vowels
[2] A, B, C, D in Hebrew
[3] Hear Israel
[4] table from which the Torah scroll is read
[5] Song concludes Passover Seder

My Father's Hands

When my dark-skinned father
died of melanoma

after laboring
on high-rises
that scar Toronto's skyline

his shirtless back
branded by the August sun

my mother handed down two possessions —
these are for *you*, she said.

I lay the items in a paper vault
of rose and violet
behind the glass pane
of my bedroom TV stand

and since that time
eight years ago
I have rarely opened the box

barring memory
from the screen-lit dark

until today
when I recover his
stainless steel watch

      band of brushed metal
      links like fish scale

      on its seafaring face,
      a glass dome
      that keeps the hour

engraved on the back
in old English font
I read:

Torino
8-15-46

he would have been eighteen
when he first saw the watch in a storefront window.

Hebraica, the Italians called the smuggled Jews
granting him free streetcar rides for his losses

from a burrow
in the Berashtan forest
the hands of the watch pointed
to a city of kindness.

Winding the watch, he listened
for the soft assurance of its tick.

*

At twenty in Barcelona
I bought a gift for my flannel-shirt father:

      a pair of cocoa brown leather gloves
      lined with cream-colored rabbit fur
      three vein-like cords at the centre

my fingers, thick fleshy stalks
glide into his gloves
their callus leather skin
furrowed by ice salt winters

yet, along the broken seams
I discover a surgical
map of cross x's
stitched by his hand
in dark brown thread.

Those same hands
that hurled half-eaten grapefruits
across the divide of our kitchen table-
bitter pith of words on his tongue

hands that gently plied the tip of a needle

to prick open a sliver
while I grit my teeth

that looped the letter 'J'
in Jakob
signing his passport name
on birthday cards.

Fatherless
he clenched fatherhood
in the burning palm of his hand.

*

Sometimes I stretch
my hands in mid-air
to measure them against his
for length and width
for their reflex
delayed capacity
to heal

After the Fire Let Out (on Rushton Road)

After the fire let out
from our neighbor's second-story bedroom,
the house stood
shamed, slurred
by the lashing tongue
of flames.

Shingles charred in coal grey,
floors unswept of ash,
a back window,
the hollow black mouth of a cave.

The woman who lived there
had been resuscitated,
her albescent skin
pinched tight to
the contours of an oxygen mask.

How still she lay,
how small,
under the white hard beams of water
shooting through the sky,
her frost silver hair, cobwebs

spun along the grey mat
ambulance stretcher.

At first, thinking her dead
I cried on the steps of our veranda.

Later, when we learned of three elements in school:
fire, air and water,
I remembered her resurrection in bloodless color:
grey, black and white.

Months afterward,
mothers strolling with their baby carriages
looked away,
hurried past
the burned-down house on Rushton Road
to ward off sudden illness,
infant crib syndrome,
the legend
of fire.

They did not bear witness.

Cocksfield Avenue

Bungalow, a crooked street
in patchwork memory.

The phantom family. Rubber tires
stockpiled on neighbor's lawn, front door, padlocked.

Around our poodle-trim bushes, this landmark: a tree trunk
painted minstrel white, casualty
of summer lightning. Crossing

Wilson Heights, school satchel in hand,
there is the panda-eyed girl in fish net-stockings, mini-skirt,
lips: flammable red, shouting down cars, while her grandfather,
exile of their peeling-blue shack, plods
up and down the road in altered time.

Cigarette in hand, Bryna chasing boys
for a misfired ball. Police
troop heaving beach-chair Bryna, trespasser
on our black tar driveway. Family secrets

run in rivulets of rain water,
leaked gas. Me, safe

behind the screen door, as Dad bounces down
the road to rescue Mrs. Swan from her husband.
Bryna squealing to the Feds about a clandestine
printing business in Mr. Cappell's basement.

His wife, Pearl, bell-tone bard
on summer porches, children rooted
around her, daisy petals open to the sun.
Pearl, shell in matte white, peering
out a rain-soaked window,
days before her passing.

Hopscotch squares on splintered
driveways; cars swerve, land
oblique in snow-filled ditches;
silver fuscia gleam of bicycle wheels in orbit;
playmates concealed in backyard
shadows; fall of dusk to snare us home.

On Cocksfield Avenue, I sound the imperfect, impermanent
tenor of our lives: round pitch pipe
pressed between my lips,
lemon rinds of melody to carry.

Legacy

I learned to question God
from a story of *Yom Kippur*[1] my mother once told
on broadloom steps that muffled sound,
her voice foggy with memory.

In the mourner's month, September, 1942
as mothers broke their water
on freight trains
that snuffed the air from the living,

Jews, in the hamlet of Osmolica,
collected a multitude of good acts and sins
and piled them high as sacrament in a wood shack.

City-reared Jews, tailor-thrift Jews,
tame and hungry *shtetl* Jews
fasting to the letter of the law,

wrung their hands in fever prayer,
tore their hair and pummeled walls,
until their Maker could taste blood.

Save us, *Gott,* they cried in Yiddish,
mother tongue culled from the pure strain of their tormentors.

Reboyne Sheloylem,[2] forgive us,
they paid homage in Hebrew.
Seal us from harm in the Book of Life.

Which language did God favor behind the gates of the Righteous?
Neither.

Whose voice did he hear?
Not one.

Except that of a child who looked on in abject terror

and in her duel with God,
stepped from the burning bush
to testify
to his seeming indifference.

[1]Day of Atonement and fasting, most solemn of Jewish holidays
[2]Almighty merciful father

Passover, 1962

No middle plank needed
to lengthen the tree
for this harvesting of family.

Our table set for five.
At the head, my father, heavy in his medieval responsibility,
pats down like anointment
a red velvet gold-trim *kippah*.[1]

Reciting verse in frays,
hanging threads on a prayer shawl,
curving words in fractions of blue,
as he must have in a low-lit *cheder* [2] in Mir
where his schoolmates wore grave piety
like premature beards,
where their eyes held the prophecy:
> Before our time
> we will sink like stones to the bottom of wells.

And we of the next generation marvel
at our father's bicycle speed.
From his mouth,
a ticker tape parade.

The sounds he makes
tapped out in Morse Code.

Platooned in the steam kitchen,
my mother urges us to sing.
Her sinew
builds a choir of symbolism for our family.

In a corner sits my high-chaired sister,
the prophet Elijah.
Next to me, my twitching brother,
whose nomad eyes wander from right to left,
never to cross the River Jordan.
Each word landing
like a pot hole on the page.

We who can neither disown or claim as our own,
flirt and skirt behind pillars of tradition
to join the ghosts seated at our table.

Through the dark lit hallway,
our voices ring of Exodus:
from Egypt
from Lublin
and Belarus.

The past papers our walls with a thin film of soot.
Sometimes, the past is a cyclone
that strikes at the center with its gathering weight.

And we face each other as we do every day
And I hear myself question as a birthright
What makes this day different from all others
Proud of the Hebrew
I can chant in toddler stages

My eyes fix on
the cartoon drawings of gold-crested Pharoh
and his curvaceous daughter
in the made-easy Hebrew *Hagaddah.*[3]

And I hear myself question as a birthright
What makes this day different from all others
Proud of the Hebrew
I can chant in toddler stages

Come Seder night,
my mother buys a wax-filled glass,
the *Jahrzeit*[4] candle,
close to extinguishing
closer to Heaven.

On the window ledge,
the cloudy cup
becomes a lantern.

Pass over this house, it says
We were spared and we are the living
Pass over

23

In secret, I feel relief.
I am not my parents.

I have
a mother, a father, a brother,
a sister.

Children slip into life preservers easily
when faced with any menace.

Outwitting harm,
they can be ruthless and shrewd
keepers of the faith.

[1] kippah: thin skullcap
[2] cheder: word in both Hebrew and Yiddish for classroom of Jewish studies
[3] Hagaddah: prayer book read during the feast of Passover
Seder: a ceremonial dinner held on the first and second days of Passover, which
includes: prayer, the eating of specified foods symbolizing the bondage of the Israelites
in Egypt, and the singing of traditional songs
[4] Jahrzeit: single day every year commemorating death of a loved one (Yiddish word,
Germanic origin)

Reading a Photograph
(On the Coming of the Shoah)

This is a Photograph of Me

It was taken some time ago.
(It is difficult to say
how large or small I am:
the effect of water
on light is a distortion)
                    —Margaret Atwood

This is a photograph
in ash white and stone grey.
A family looms centre
secluded in a summer forest,
Poland, 1937.

Seven children sprout like stems.

I trace serrated lines along the border -
faded scar tissue along pelvic bone.

At the back, time inscribed in roman numerals. Addressee:
Dear Loved Ones. Did the photo cross
the ocean to pre-war Palestine?

In the front row, Uncle Heniek,
at one, propped by grandmother

Devorah's steady frame. Her fingers
gently anchoring him.
Hands folded on cue,

his oval face,
an effigy
impressed on pages
of recurring summers.

Far-left and abandoned,
hammock where he once
slept with his mother: summer's

premonition of their death.
October 14, 1942.

There, against pitch black: tall knobby pines
testify to a family's bond.

In the last row, equidistant,
my gruff maternal great-grandmother, Tammy
presides over her progeny of twenty
in a dark v-neck dress.

Widow, merchant and mother of eight,
her torso expands into a shapeless mass.

A band of sons roll up their sleeves in communion
Wives and sisters link in their summer prints
as an unmarried daughter sports a floral tie.

The soles of tread-upon shoes turn sideways.
Bruises rise up a young girl's ankles,
grass gathering at her feet.

Is she, Chana, dreaming of the river
on the opposite end of the woods?

Cradled on lap,
a first-born son
nestles in a white blanket.

Mid-row, Grandfather Eleazar kneels,
tight-lipped before the Teutonic Age,

his jaw taut with inevitability.

Didn't he, hour upon hour, sing *Kinderjohren*,[1]
thread its somber melody
into weaves of wool?

In striped pajamas,
his surviving child, my mother, Roza,
teases the prosthetic
glass eye of the camera.

Chamber of collective
memory through which
I read this picture —
vanished generations.

[1]Yiddish song: "Childhood Years"

Family Portrait

You and I rest in the stationary frame
of a family portrait.

Into that glossy version,
we revert, time-warped,
in pre-ordained shapes and sizes.

You, pegged the reliable square,
I, the deviate oblong.
To whom did we devote the radius of a circle?

I squirm into undersized shoes
You contract your limbs
as we collide on that habitual plane.

Negatives of our past selves
under a tungsten light.

Still, we return again
to dust the family portrait,
by whose idiom we can't help but be defined.

To hold it like a suspended chord
and dream it back in black and white.

Film Reel: Crystal Beach, Ontario

Crystal white sand
and cherry coke waves
in a flush of rose color.

Rib-like ridges of earth,
a sonography
under shallow water.

Baby sister lies
on a pink inflatable raft
with tubes the shape of rigatoni.

Her plump legs rock the air
in a jig of independence.

On her left, brother kneels,
his protective shadow covering her heart like a patch.

Peering at the camera for its constancy,
he smiles, toothless.

Cushioned by the warm mud floor of the lake,
I rest my thimble hands,

shield of small things,
on the plastic raft

and tilt my face toward Linda
as she lifts her head at the water's rupture.

The infant who can't fathom density,
trusting our love
without weighing its mass.

On the Meaning of Chanukah

In the age of the Maccabees,
a single day's worth of oil
burned in the Temple for eight whole days,
read the teacher.

The oil couldn't have sustained light and heat
for so many hours, a student argued.

Can a man's hope and faith be measured with any accuracy?

No. But a man's faith can be shaken
like the apple on a branch of a tree.

And is yours so easily shaken?

It has been, as is true for most of us.

The teacher then lit a match,
and invited the student to imagine
its flame signified some intangible good
he could aspire to.

The student watched intently

as the flame bonfired,
receded. Went out.

Having witnessed the
predictability
of science, he was not
yet convinced
of the teacher's meaning.

But sometime later,
the student remembered the flame
and the buoyant belief he had invested in its brief light.

A belief he had stored in the Ark of his soul
to secure there as a covenant.

It was then he decided the flame
was a symbol he could understand.

Parchment of Peace

Say the word land in a single breathless syllable.
Soon a multitude of words, dense and dislocated,
crowd around like jockeying spectators
at a match to the bloody death.

Border Territory Settlement Occupation

The words clamor on hilltops, collide
and clash on consecrated ground
God alone could not grace.

Say the promise of land: say it in full
with sustenance and serenity.

The promise is ancient; the promise is new.

We must call in a grand and divine landlord
who can measure the slopes of these hills,
surmise the stone's age in these walls and towers,
who can check every crevice
and leave no patch of solemn earth unturned.

Who can mandate the rightful owner of this land
called both by its maiden and married name?

Its past and present, a spiral of yearning
fulfilled and forgotten, redressed and redeemed.

A vessel for the dispossessed
to hold in abeyance.

Settle this land, so it can breathe
in soft pulsating waves
over parchments of sand.

Read this land like a handwritten scripture
Reinvented from an older tome.

Bracha – A Blessing

I keep my ear tuned to the humming of the wire,
low to the grooming ground.

I am a child of the Diaspora, long fathered
by the promise of cumulative good.

Perhaps, an answer will come
hidden in the predictable verbatim of daily life.

Perhaps, it will offer itself up, clear,
succinct as the hand of the noon-day hour,

when words will curve like calligraphy in air,
calling me out by name.

If an answer should come,
will I have the courage to claim it?

II.

Ballast

You call it a kind of leakage —
plasma of the blood —
as if our skin was lined
with erasable rubber.

The script on our faces
transparent. How I wish

I could grow in a kingdom
of shade, climbing
like ivy.
The rocks would be my ballast,
and from the walls I scale,
I would watch,
paying no tariff
as a lineage of gardeners changes hands.

Feeding the Ducks

Preserved: two park benches, three
park tables, narrow perimeter
of grass and cropped bush.
On the opposite end of the pond,
grand-tiered houses on stilts.
A bronze plaque —
'Old Village of Thornhill.'

At the edge of grass,
the little girl tilts forward,
a paperweight sail, her pink
skin evenly covered in level
15 sun screen. Stretching
her arm over the water,
she disperses alms,
bread over Galilee.

Choreographing from the bench
behind, her father snaps
a photograph, playing overseer
in their charity, playing
coach in her aim for ducks.
"Tear off smaller pieces.
Pull back to pitch farther," he directs —

the little girl gesticulates
in sullen afternoon heat.

A nonchalant duck approaches. Soon
another. As if
by trumpet call,
a white procession
of duck brethren make their way
towards the little girl,
screeching geek geek in the pollinated air.

Heady in power,
the little girl throws kisses —
pellets of bread into the gulping
mouths of ducks

who tread close,
and after the last scattering,
form rings around the smooth
sphere of sky on water.

Lull

See how I build my cocoon
of bamboo and brittle leaves.

How I spin this silk-lined web
far off in a corner. You are

a witness; my heart's stone silence
bears live proof of damage. Morning

dew rises like a vapor, opaque
as a veil of fog.

We walk barefoot
to the edge of a weather-worn deck,
and wait
in shared silence to sound the tuning fork
of serenity sustained across a summer lake
soft over bands of dark green onyx.

Do you sense how like a fledgling bird
I can fall in the limber space between us?

Each breath a lull
in the pulse of confidences.

Row Me Out on Blue Mountain Lake

Row me out where mountains climb
to a bluer vista,

where titan pine and yellow birch
are dwarfed
on the face of water,

where oars dip,
nursing calm across a silk sheet lake

as a heron wakes
the marshland grass, ruffles

a tribe of cattails, stirring
hope from its dormant nest.

Row me out under a purple
pennant sky, dusk
deepening on an easy glide.

When the moon vanishes,
a silver coin in the palm of night,

we will pull back our hands,

constrict our hearts a little
at the steady
attenuation
of days.

I Dream of Trees in Their Female Form

I dream of trees in their female form -

Hip sway of branches
baring stone pit fruit

Milk flesh stems
in the cycle of blooms

Plum skin peeled
under ardent sun

Brush of rust gold taffeta
across a fall leaf floor

Wood dress mannequins
in spring pose

color, and in their most intimate
season, how trees,
heartwood and limb,
shed
all reserve
under the ice white
blanket of winter's sky.

A Boy Dreams of a Fishing Rod
(at the Plattsburgh, New York, Marina)

Seagulls in flight balk from a distance. A black boy in lime swim trunks dips a cottonwood branch into the water. He is waiting for minnows. Or a small perch like the one the woman near the edge of the grass has caught and thrown away. "Too small," she says, as she rests on the smooth back of a rock.

Lapping water smacks the decayed molar of a tree trunk. A locus of mayflies circle the fisherwoman's head.

Soon, the little boy is holding two branches, waving the soft poplar rods over the water like biblical staffs. Mining a fisherman's skill, he swings them backward and forward above his head to cast his lure.

The world around him is moving, waiting in a story circle. Six brown-speckled ducks form a signature line on wavy water. A blue and white schooner floats feet away from the dock, tugging at the chain like a pedigreed pet. Poles spearhead the white meringue skies. A car idles in the parking lot, its driver's right ear pinned to his cell phone to hear over the rasp and wheeze of the engine. A young woman in the café stands on the doorstep, elbows crossed, waiting for customers and the belated promise of summer. Voices echo in a beam of sound and fade.

The little boy reels in his imaginary fish and runs, hands outstretched, to his mother, lolling in the grass.

View From a Not-too-Distant Bridge
(Heath Park, Toronto)

Two school-age bikers, perched
high on pear-shaped seats, swerve
around a bend, disappear
in a swirl of dust, gravel
cracking under their wheels.

A jogger enters from a hidden
dip in the valley, throwing
heavyweight punches at neutral air.

Mud-brown telephone poles line the road
as crucifixes.

Gauze clouds float
across the screen sky. I squint
at the cowardly sun that sticks
on the panel like a stain of white glue.

Across a bridge, a biker spins
into a dream of Dorothy's, and I hear
the wicked witch cackle, my pretty,
as the strings play pizzicato
over a sun-dry Kansas cornfield.

All too soon,
the bicyclist is cut from the scene,
and pictures dissolve,
tea spoons of salt in a water cup.

My feet follow the shake
and rumble of the Spadina line:
projector light flashing in a darkened tunnel,
clip speed of a train chasing
window-size trees, past
slanting tombstone hilltops,
bungalows in cereal box rows.
Toronto's cityscape tamed
into submission.

III.

Breaking Vows in a Telephone Booth

Walking on Bloor Street,
I saw
an icon in white,
an angel on sabbatical,
wings trapped
in the straitjacket bodice of a red telephone booth.

There stood a nun in the crowning of her habit,
the tread of her veil sailing around my iris -
white capsized by
brown sandaled toes
her ear on the receiver,
her back to me,
and on the Western Wall,
a poster sounded a percussive
cymbal in my agnostic
deliberating heart,
ringing in my ears
with a precision prick of irony.

Waiting till she squirmed her way out of the lair of graffiti,
out of the stale exposed grime of that public booth
with its coin receptacle

and its shredded hanging version
of the Urban Book of Genesis,
I, playing the dybbuk,
followed behind her steps as she crossed the pedestrian green,
a triplet of mischief notes tapping on my brain.

Whispering what I read in the nun's shadow,
I teased and toyed with the sacrilegious slogan,
playing catch with the smoke cloud of movie dialogue
floating over the lover's head.

"Commitment," the poster read:
"Commitment can really suck the life out of you."

Narnia

Friday afternoon,
school books stashed
in dungeon drawers.

Crayon fingers trace epithets
carved on yellow wood
desk tops.

Perched above us,
Mrs. Granger wears glasses to read.
On her rims,
a gold-purple crocus budding east and west.

Storybook in hand,
her voice glides
over clouds of chalk dust,
circling round our
unrepentant day dreams.

Pages flip like tapering wings
as Lucy enters
the wardrobe of running imagination,
steps into crystal cakes of snow
the numb slumbering winter of Narnia.

On the second Friday,
cubes of Turkish delight stain
our pink tongues.

On Friday the good,
King Aslan splayed on a stone table,
heart spliced by the witch's knife.

Can sacrifice come from a promise?

Wardrobes tempt me still.
I wade through dark suffocating fur,

resist the burn and chafe of wool
to land breathless
nascent at the open
border of a story.

An uncrowned queen
in the realm of invention

The Myth of Cleopatra

We plunder the musty cavern
of mother's dresser drawer
for beads and baubles in jellyfish colors,
a drove of dip-dyed pearls hanging low,
for starfish broaches of glass
that prick our royal fingers.

Trailing sheets of
white and lavender thread,
our gossamer robes,
we make the procession
of a plumaged bird, the sacred Ibis,
along the length of the bedchamber,

the low-lying Nile
of birth and betrayal.

Antony's name drifting like frankincense
over the impromptu chatter of child talk,
over the lilt of sister sounds
in her dynasty:
Alexandria, Lydia and Syria.

We purr on soft paws, crown
soprano Caesar's name,

and hold high the myth of Cleopatra,
like premature bearers of
ageless femininity.

Self-appointed paper queens,
how little we understood
the grip of her womanhood -
the sly soft intimations.

Her seduction,
a snake's path
to a well of pleasure.

Teaching ESL
(at a Branch of Shopper's World)

I greet the faces of my students
on the ice tip of the 21st century,
in a tower of Babel
(a branch of Shopper's World
in Northern Etobicoke)
within walking distance of high-rise
ghettoes for the dislocated.

Outside classrooms,
young and old men huddle
in brotherhoods of leisure,
backs against obsolete storefronts.

I venture into the phonetic den,
tongue and teeth tripping over
consonant clusters, spattering
surnames like melon seeds.

On the seventh day,
I recreate phonemes on black boards
as my students retrieve meaning like a bone
and bring-it-back-Rover.

I attach a finder's fee
in the form of a word
and chain it to a tree.
Because they must later recover the word
in order to call it learning.

Occasionally, I drip dry
the color from our lives
With my white chalk pellets,
pull out the arsenal:
the YES-NO questions
the infamous 'do' prong,

and flashing a gallery of visual aids -
mug shots, I prod and cue.

Until their eyes
flash in recognition — a moonbeam
across thin lifeless walls.

Until their mouths
curve in satisfaction,
and they shout out,
and their arms bob up,
like winners at a local Bingo game.

Pirates, we dig up gold - the stem of words
and barter in *lingua franca.*

Surgeons of syntax,
we repair language
with needle and thread.

And when we conjugate
past and present, we sense
how our lives move one tense to another,
turning over and back again like a coda
around this undefeated planet.

Little Red Riding Hood in the Writing Classroom

Computers marooned against the plaster wall.
Desks lined in gridlock rows.
Learners stare ahead,
train commuters
passing through a tunnel.

At the first sign of white,
eyes dart up at the blackboard.
In the left-hand column:
Perrault's 16th century guide on courtly manners.
In the right-hand column:
the Brothers' Grimm code of morals.

Leaping across the Franco-Prussian border
(and centuries in between),
the heroine/émigré of the fairy tale keeps her invincible red cap.

We empty our basket of symbols and archetypes,
when Natalie dives into her backpack
on a private expedition.

Her cheeks and ears burn flamingo.

Snatching a little red book from out of the wolf's
lair, she disappears, her blonde head cropped
behind the cover.

Today, I think, her defiance flashes in the family of red;
Natalie taunts with the *muleta*[1] of the rebel schoolgirl.

Days before, her weapon was a pair of scissors:
snip cut-ting the handout in 2/4 time.

Her small white hands steal authority;
paint a blush of shame on my cheeks.

I cut her forbidden journey short, this impersonator
of the fairy tale character, and demand
obedience in Brothers Grimm fashion.

All the while wondering
which character I've become.

The voice of the wolf goads me: *The way she turns the pages
of her little red book. What lovely hands she has …*

I frame her image — that axis of self
and text in my picture book of poems. And note
how unkind a symmetry we three make:
storybook heroine, classroom rebel ... me.

[1]small red cape

A Lesson in Phonetics

The hostess, bolstered on her right
by her husband, pulls full rank with her ceremony
of linen, serviettes like epaulettes, gold-plated
armory flanked by ivory-bone china.

She tells her dinner guests of a former live-in-nanny,
a woman from the Philippines, one of many
who pledge their homage to the Maple leaf
with paper towels and scouring pads, who charter
the Canadian anthem as lullabies to the newborn.

Driving her employee home, the hostess pried,
"Are you still married?" "No," the nanny answered.
"He bit me." "He bit you?"
The words struck at the windowpane like hail — three times the
    intruder
"Where?" the hostess hounded on a blood mission.

Miming assault, the Philippino woman bounced
in the seat like a rag doll, memory
congealed in her body.

"Oohh," interrupted the hostess.

"He b-e-a-t you. Well, don't you think of staying with him,"
she counseled
in her faultless tongue.

Laughter spills across the dinner table;
condescension
tossed like spare change.

*

The phonetician might present a different slant
on this discrimination of vowels.
Though both are monopthongs,
the lax vowel "I" in "bit" occurs only in a closed syllable
while its counterpart,
the tense vowel "I" in "beet'
is more versatile,
occurring in both
a closed and open syllable.

I might add that either vowel would force
the speaker or the doer of the action
to bare his or her front teeth.

Critique

He tossed grains of truth —
the department head of creative writing.
I echoed back phrases —
a yellow parakeet on his shoulder.

Repeating words
that burst like helium balloons
with every slash of his pen-knife.

Watching him string up
antiquated lines
through an open window.

Decoding in
small
cursive script
what he thought I ought to say.

Yet ... the lines
he rewrote sat on the page
like the backside of a hefty man
who finally finds a place to sit
on a streetcar
in the deadweight
heat
of July.

The Art of Conversation

When speaker 'A' saw speaker 'B'
for all intents and purposes
B's face was barely reminiscent,
but that fact was superfluous

The two began an oiled routine
of instant body gestures
and utterances that swirled and swayed
in mannered stress and textures

Offering coated pleasantries
like bonbons in a box
Faithful to the lines prescribed
Each turn-of-phrase well-stocked
They hesitated and cajoled
pretended set alarm
Their slight retractions from the truth
minimized the harm

If either one was called upon
to deal the tactic's game
They kept relations in good stead
and courteously remained
Friends, and if not friends, then

acquaintances for certain
(Though logically that attribute
can't favor such a person)

Thus, 'A' and 'B' cordially engaged
in rounds of pitter patter
And 'A' and 'B' kept ions from
the heart core of the matter
Their converse fell on neighboring ears
on sympathetic strollers
who judged their liaison to be
in solid working order

Reading Braille

Few words left today — I've dispensed them
like so many tablets. Grown bone-weary

with our cargo of words that cumber
the tongue, our sealed promises pried open
on docks of heated
departure.

Metaphor and simile are poor intermediaries. When I last read

the strangeness of your words to me,
I stumbled across the page, fingers
tapping the raised dots. I imagine

it must be something like reading
Braille for the first time.

Nightfall on a Brooklyn Stoop
(Park Slope, 1988)

I

5 p.m. humidity muffles the mouth of the lion city.

The cool and incorporated swing turnstile doors
  to bottle-necked avenues baking in the sun.

High-heeled girls and button-brown men stagger
  on steam-press pavements, their silk ties and cotton hems
    fluttering over subway grates in a gust
      of metallic air. Soon, they train
        tunnel below where daylight buries its head

inert till the two-tone bell
  when they leap out of cars like stowaways
    climb flights of runaway stairs to wide
      tree-lined streets dappled in sun.

II

Neighbors stretch on foamy spring kitchen chairs
  plastic rickety beach chairs.

Men in undershirts

exercise their masculinity swatting mosquito air
 with thick killing hands.

Children
 abandon street games, disappear into numbered doors
 swallowing sound whole.

Dusk falls on telescopic stars
 on lantern-lit stoops

covering clouds in black sheer
 and high satin gloves.

III

Brownstones like stately squires bear
 their coat-of-arms: spiked iron fences,
  gable-shaped rooftops and pinpoint attics.

Rows of elm trees sway to the strum
 of a renegade wind. Night watchmen
  alert to the pending rain.

From an open window
across the way, a woman sings
 up and down domino scales
  in vibraphone
   triads, in the sad swirl of an oboe.

Sitting still on a Brooklyn stoop
 I listen
   long into the night, her bodiless voice
    calling me out to witness

    the fiction of a younger America.

Stevie Wonder

For one thing, it's your boyish charm
The way you ask: Can I play? Can I play?
My body answers YES in a speakeasy swing:
Play play.

Vowels open like kites
Diphthongs glide on a runway of notes
Melody and harmony bind umbilical.

You bite into sweet and sour apples
of rhythm and blues
Gift us with orchards
of song under a jazz sun. Beat the backbone

bass line rhythm for city folk growing
out of their clothes, their spaces
too tight, too wide, too small, too tall.

Jab the slide chromatic and I'll pucker my lips
Shoo-be-doo-be-doo-be-doo-da-day
I got eyes for you, Stevie
I got eyes for you.

Brooke on her Birthday

Dusk, a dull opaque grey.
Kitchen light spills across the oak wood floor
and is suspended at her feet.

Snug on a couch, legs folded,
she is a Buddha of the living room,
littered with stripped dolls, a three-wheeler
and the gutted remains of a computer.

In her left hand, she holds a soft-covered book
pour une jeune fille
its spine bent,
its pages dog-eared,
her fingers, firm and suppliant.

With her right hand,
she choreographs
the plot. *Pour expliquer.*
Her voice is steady, suffused
with feeling, wiser
than the heroine will be.

The Anglo r's roll like a trilling bird.

This is recitation, a public reading
to expectant students,
to a younger
sister, to no one at all
in the grey room.

Hush … Listen …
c'a lui fait plaisir.

We Three Sisters (for the Brontës)

We live in quiet solitude
near a vast and sullen moor
attending to our Reverend Father
who ministers the rule.

Wind-swept chimney overhead
Harsh the Vicar's temper
Yet come the summer
hills rebound
in purple robes of heather.

His parsonage by custom stands
Our lives are thinly sheltered
The story, the verse, the Gothic tale
will be for now unwelcomed.

A circle of three we needlepoint
and self-fulfill the brew
And soon a world of rising dreams
Fills up the written page.

If you should read a chapter
of this, our expertise
Affairs of the given heart
You'd guess, the novel is our trade.

A Woman of Visible Parts

What becomes visible
in summoning desire
for passion to be kindled
then peel in smoke and cinder?

How soon do eyes detect, idolize, reject
her sculpted bone and skin
of lucent porcelain
when fullness of her mouth
elicited devout
worshipping of love.

In which alchemist den
did potion first begin
to brew and stir until
it wore its magic thin?

What becomes visible
in summoning desire?
You ask to ask in vain
how passion can expire
To love the visible parts
can tax a human heart.

I am a woman, she cries,
this rich and royal hue
glows not from what is outward forged
but hidden from full view.

I Bear These Arms

I bear these arms sometimes like shields
and wage my battles till someone yields
With these same arms, I hold on tight
Nothing prepares you for what love can do

I bear these arms pinned to my sides
Can I ask you to bring them back to life?
I've policed them
need to release them
Before I'm frozen in these heights

I bear these arms
I'll move them closer
So much gone under
Buried in the past

As for the hunger
Can't say I've tamed it
But now the smallest wonder
Can bring me back

Last night, I dreamed you were my lost angel
Watching over me, answering my prayers
But you're not windblown

You're flesh and blood
I recognize love when you are near

I bear these arms sometimes like shields
and wage my battles till someone yields
With these same arms, I open up
Nothing prepares you for what love can do
Nothing prepares you for love

No Zealots Here

Be wary of blood-red banners,
of flags that burn on paragon heights,
of zealots who cry
witness words for the millennia.

Though you are drawn to the promise
of a path clairvoyant,
beguiled by vertigo lights
flooding down from above.

Remain, rather, the amateur fighter
on a platform that shifts.
Your brawn heart at cross signals,

your two-fisted brain
still battling the cost.

Choosing a Career

I took a Myers-Briggs test.
Her tone was decidedly curt.
"As per my expertise," she said,
Your scales read introvert.

One career that comes to mind,
to which you'd be best suited
is cosmetologist or beautician."
With that, she short concluded.

"I'm partial towards counseling."
"You have the sensibility,
but then again, you'd need to curb
your strain of vulnerability."

"I could be less abstract,
might solicit for the law."
"Your logic then must supersede
imagination's draw.

Forget entrepreneurship,
You don't score as promotional.
Don't think of working with machines
You're low on motor visual.

Neither should you buy or sell
or hustle any trade."
She shook her head from left to right
as if to punctuate.

"I've considered academia."
"What, work towards a doctorate?"
"Tried my hand at pulp fiction."
"The novel turned conglomerate?

Of glamour, money, melodrama
in dizzying colored panorama!"

"A journalist, perhaps?"
"You must curtail, be terse.
And lose this penchant you possess
for uncommunicative verse."

My elusive search was halted
to study mother tongue
and navigate across the page
the words that tumble run.

I did not color fingernails
in deep Aruba blue,
but taught and schooled and learned on par
to stroke the sentence true.

And so I take my final leave
from these infringing voices.
Ending my quest for dozen more
ill-matched career choices.

My conclusion is not deep.
My answers less profound.
My advice, though, is well-steeped
in experience, I found.

It's best to clear retire
from harboring an ear
to what others may conspire
when choosing a career.

Pursuit

I offer you nothing
more than a poem, a pledge

on fractured faith. I pursued
the poem for some time, though

I have made efforts to conceal
the strike of mallet -

sound; sympathy. The pluck
and string of words

that rebound; the spill of powder blue
for the still shot sky;

and those running feet you heard?
It was me, chasing

phrases through a maze, me, alone,
mounting lines

like weight-bearing beams across the roof
of these verses.

Acknowledgements

Special thanks to Michael Carrino for his generous support in fine-tuning this collection.

My gratitude, as well, to readers over time who lent their skill: to Kenneth Sherman, Karen Shenfeld, and Ellen Jaffe.

"Choosing a Career"; "We Three Sisters (for the Bronte Sisters)"; and "Stevie Wonder" were published in *Rhythm Poetry Magazine* 2 (3) (Spring /Summer of 2010).

"Narnia" was the winner of Toronto Reading Council Poetry Contest, Spring 2008.

"Lull" was published in *Arborealis: A Canadian Anthology of Poetry* (Thornhill: The Ontario Poetry Society, 2008).

"A Lesson in Phonetics" appeared in *Women in Judaism: A Multidisciplinary Journal* 5 (1) (Winter 2008).

"Teaching ESL" appeared in *English Quarterly* 34 (1,2) (2002).

"Passover, 1962" was published in *Parchment* (1999).

"On the Meaning of Hanukkah" won the *Canadian Jewish News* Award for Poetry, December, 1997

"Breaking Vows in a Telephone Booth" was published in *Paper Salad Poetry Journal* 3 (1992).

Photo credit: John Mitchell

Carol Lipszyc earned a Doctorate of Education in 2006 at the Ontario Institute for Studies in Education/University of Toronto. Before teaching English language arts throughout Toronto, Carol was a professional singer with Canadian television and radio appearances to her credit. Her ESL/Literacy Reader, *People Express,* was published by Oxford University Press in 1996. Select poems, prose, and book reviews have been published in *Parchment, Midstream, English Quarterly,* and *Canadian Woman Studies/les cahiers de la femme.* Educational articles have appeared in *The Quest For Meaning: Narratives of Teaching, Learning and the Arts* (Sense Publishers) and *The Camp Narratives of Internment and Exclusion* (Cambridge Scholars). Carol is currently an Assistant Professor at the State University of New York (SUNY), Plattsburgh, teaching English Teacher Education and Creative Writing.

Marquis Book Printing Inc.

Québec, Canada
2010

Printed on Silva Enviro 100% post-consumer EcoLogo certified paper,
processed chlorine free and manufactured using biogas energy.

WEIGHTS & MEASURES

WEIGHTS & MEASURES

Miriam N. Kotzin

Weights & Measures

Copyright © 2009

by Miriam N. Kotzin

Cover art by Peter Groesbeck

Cover design by Lucy Swerdfeger

Published by

~Star Cloud Press®~
6137 East Mescal Street
Scottsdale, Arizona 85254-5418

ISBN: 978-1-932842-36-4 — $12.95

Library of Congress Control Number: 2009923147

Printed in the United States of America

To My Parents
Dr. Isadore Kotzin
Frances Scheiber Kotzin

Table of Contents

CEREMONIES

ELEVATED RISKS

WEIGHTS & MEASURES

Ceremonies

TEA CEREMONIES IN WINTER

"They flee from me, that sometime did me seek,
With naked foot stalking within my chamber."
                                    Sir Thomas Wyatt

1.
We sit, polite. The cup of tea grows cold.
The painted china's thin. The cloth is white
and smooth. The silver's polished. We've grown old
apart, both wary of another slight.

The cup of tea grows cold. And while we speak
of this and that, we watch the twilight sink
into the lake. The evening drowns. No streak
of light is left in sky or lake. I shrink,

for while we speak the background music plays
that very song to which we danced so long
ago. You have forgotten. Then you raise
your cup and sip the tea grown cold. I'm wrong.

The background music plays. You just pretend
you do not know this tune or mark its end.

2.
You do not know this tune or mark its end
by any gesture when the music slides,
gives way to the next Musaked song. Attend
the overwhelming question that presides

unasked. Or don't. It doesn't matter now.
I've seen that you remember. Plum preserves
and currant jam and clotted cream allow,
facilitate, a sweetened silence. Nerves—

it doesn't matter how—can make us say
what we would not, like careless silverware
upon a china plate. You seem blasé,
but it's too late to say you cannot care.

What makes us speak, or keeps us silent, still
as this, the frozen cricket on the sill?

3.
As this, the frozen cricket on the sill,
becomes an emblem, so the gaudy night
in silken skirts appears to send a chill,
a hint that longer dark lurks out of sight.

Since I am moved to metaphor, then I
might tell you all about my rise and fall
—a bobbin's passive progress—with a sigh.
If I were moved to speech, would that be all?

And I can see the waiter standing near
our table. If he should want us to go
so he can have this lake-side four-top clear
for dinner, he will subtly let us know.

The waiter standing near us looks to see
if we have given up on having tea.

4.
If we have given up on having tea,
then have we given up on giving up?
You've left your scone half-eaten. Fidgety,
you shift your weight, and peer into your cup.

On having tea that's cold and weak, you look
across the table, where I sit, and slide
your chair away. You hold your pocketbook
as though you want to pay. You say, "I tried."

That's also cold and weak. You look as though
you want some words to change your mind. The key
to your engagement won't be found, I know,
with ease in this our cobbled comity.

And then, aloud, I say, "That's cold and weak,"
four words we're both surprised to hear me speak.

MIRIAM N. KOTZIN

5.
Four words. We're both surprised to hear me speak
like that. You say, "You never had respect
for what I thought or felt. That's your technique
for handling me, dismissive for effect."

"Do speak your mind," I say. I aimed at wit
and irony, but missed. I see your eyes
grow wide, then nearly close. "Yes, I admit
that wasn't kind," I add. "Don't patronize,"

you say. "Do speak your mind," I say again
in softer tones. In fact, it's true I would
not wish to patronize—no gentleman
would care to stoop to that. I understood.

I repeat, but smile, "Please. Speak your mind.
I've no intent at all to be unkind."

6.
"I've no intent at all to be unkind,"
I say again. "No doubt it comes to you
with ease so you don't have to think to find
the words," you say. You're speaking like a shrew.

"So I'm unkind? Just look at who's not nice
right now? Let's stop. Why do we have to fight?
You're looking for some way, for some device
to keep me distant." Pause. "Isn't that right?"

"So I'm not nice! That's it! That's what I mean.
The little girl's not being nice. Bad girl!
The little girl's not nice. She's being seen
and heard." You catch your breath. "I'm not your pearl."

"What are you, then, if not a precious gem?"
Au bout, this is a last-ditch stratagem.

7.
Au bout, this is a last-ditch stratagem
that does not work. I wonder what the right
words are: if only I could think of them.
I came with hope. I didn't want to fight.

I have to smile when I catch sight of our
reflection in the window glass. We seem
like any happy couple there, an hour
to pass in rented luxury. A gleam

of our lost selves, reversed, is what I see
illuminated on the glass in light
that flickers. Watching you I think, "You flee
from me." The rest is lost: the lines take flight.

And so I'm left with nothing to withhold.
We sit, polite. The cup of tea grows cold.

MIRIAM N. KOTZIN

THE RINGS

We chose our wedding rings with care:
mine, gold waves; his, wide chain-like link—
hands, lives joined, such a perfect pair.
We chose our wedding rings with care,
our lives gleaming. How unaware
we were. We never thought to think.
We chose our wedding rings with care:
mine, gold waves; his, wide chain-like link.

HONEYMOON BEACH PLACE

From here they have a microscopic view
of sky and sea, but they are satisfied
for now with what they have, and they'll make do
together, honeymooning now beachside.
This week they find it easy to agree
to plan their days without a strategy:
how late to sleep, and what to eat and when:
and when to swim, and sun, and love again.

And once, for three whole frantic hours she
believes that she has lost her wedding ring.
She knows she hasn't dropped it in the sand
or had it slip unnoticed in the sea.
He says to make it better that he'd fling
away his band. She studies her bare hand.

7 MIRIAM N. KOTZIN

LAUNDRY

The clothes you tossed aside are just laundry
to me. Your shirts, and socks, and briefs are free
to mingle with my bras and sweats. They're mine
to deal with, heaped in piles. So by design
I measure soap and bleach. Lint-free,

they'll tumble dry: a hot, moist ribaldry
of sleeves and straps, of tangled dungaree
and twisted sheets. All these now intertwine:
the clothes you tossed aside.

The petty details of housewifery—
to sort, pre-treat and wash—my battery
of skills deployed.   Tonight the opened wine,
left breathing by our bed, will wait for us. Mine,
the clothes you tossed aside.

How We Leave

We leave the bed
with rumpled covers tossed aside.
We leave the bed
long past the sky, once streaked with red,
has paled to morning's blue, for I'd
become in turn virgin, whore, bride.
We leave the bed.

MIRIAM N. KOTZIN

DISHES

The dirty dishes in the kitchen sink
are last night's dinner's and our morning cups
of coffee that you brought to bed. I think
the dirty dishes in the kitchen sink
include those cups you brewed for us to drink
(I always call them loving cups).
The dirty dishes in the kitchen sink
are last night's dinner's and our morning cups.

TEMPLE ORANGES

This morning I watch you peel
a temple orange, ripe and sweet.
This morning I watch you peel
and section, juice dripping, and eat
a temple orange, ripe and sweet.
Watching, I feel my heart beat,
a temple orange, ripe and sweet.

This, your morning meal,
your sweetened fingers dripping,
This, your morning meal
after our love making
I watch you stand and peel.
I watch, remembering
your sweetened fingers dripping.

The word's too weak, "sweet,"
to name how you peel and wring
and section, juice dripping, and eat.
The word's too weak, "sweet,"
after our love making,
to name our morning meal,
to name how you peel and wring.

Miriam N. Kotzin

BEACH HOUSE

They chose this house so they could hear the waves
at night. All day the sea could churn; the wind
might whip the flag against the pole; the sand
would rise in blowing veils and, swirling, tear
or move along the beach, dissolve like sheets
of fog or like another useless lie.

They would have sworn that they would never lie,
as those who lie will swear with ease. She waves
away her doubts and buys new shams and sheets
in peach and green. She hangs a flowered wind
sock from a branch. She learns new crafts: to tear
and wrap, to dye, to layer colored sand

in bottles, making new bright worlds and sand-
cast candles, polished stones. And then she'd lie
in bed and read *Gourmet*, and plan to tear
out recipes to try next week in waves
of hope that broke to old regrets. She'd wind
up making something quick and iron sheets

and practice fancy napkin folds. Then sheets
of rain. She walks out on the sodden sand
alone and wraps herself in rain and wind,
a chosen cloak. She had no need to lie:
he hadn't asked her where or why. The waves
of Tennyson, she thinks, amazed to tear

the pages open: "idle tears." "A tear
is just a tear, as time goes" wrong. Dry sheets
(Egyptian cotton, thread count high) in waves;
her thoughts, like lost Perseids shower: "Sand
and sun, a world of fun, a living lie—
I hang my laundry out to dry in wind.

I quilt and quill and know the way to wind
a watch (a useless skill with quartz). I tear,
not cut, the lettuce, spin it dry. I lie
quite still. I write on linen-finish sheets
and do not phone. I smile. I sweep up sand.
I am the perfect mermaid wife of waves."

Her words fly off on wind, like newsprint sheets.
She hadn't hoped to see a tear in clouds. Cold sand.
"He won't lie," she thinks, turns to home, and waves.

Miriam N. Kotzin

BACK

Back, they throw the blankets to the floor
in aqua waves on the sisal rug. Their bodies
cool from the outside shower, hair dripping,
mermaid, fisher, they make a show of slow
stripping, dropping their wet suits where they
stand like new strangers, staring across the vast
and unfamiliar bed.

      And she knows they'll lie
all night on sandy sheets while the wind
lifts the white curtains in slow billows and
carries the distant hushing of the waves
and she will lie awake and remember
another summer's distant clang of rigging
and listen for the tires of a certain solitary car
as he lies and sleeps.

      And he knows that she
will lie awake and listen to his even
breathing as he lies on his side and he
watches the curtains billow while he
thinks how in the street below them
the mist must hang in the headlights
of passing cars. And that she will surely
accept his sleep like a well-earned gift.

IMPRESSIONISM ON THE BEACH

"The violet shadows in the sand
are like the paintings of Monet,"
you said. "I mean haystacks, the play
of light." I thought, "Just take my hand.

"You can be clever, see things, and
 still kiss." Once more I hear you say,
"The violet shadows in the sand
are like the paintings of Monet."

"Hold still. The sun does not. We stand
and watch the waves. Our *Dejeuner
sur l'herbe*, this. You're overdressed, a
dark-suited man. But that's Manet."
"The violet shadows in the sand..."

Miriam N. Kotzin

GHOST CRABS

We chose a night the moon was full
to hunt ghost crabs. Our flashlights swept
the sand to find the crabs. We kept
small distance as we watched them pull

their prey apart. In films we see
a sanitized repast of beast on beast:
the tiger with gazelle as feast
presented from afar. Now we

can hear the plover's peep
and watch the frantic flap of wing
and track the messy trail, the ring
of blood that's left behind to seep

into the sand. And when all's done
we go back home unsatisfied.
With what dark force have we allied
to watch a kill for fun?

SHORELINE

I can do nothing about the way
the sun slowly fell into the bay
or about the pink and silver glaze
that shimmered and then rose as a haze
above the beach only yesterday.

About the light that wavered like moiré
I wore once long ago, pink and gray,
elusive as a forgotten phrase,
I can do nothing.

We carried our shoes, careless as a
drunken bridesmaid dangling her bouquet.
The bay before us turned first to baize
then lead. Like equivocating praise,
sanderlings maneuvered. I heard you say,
"I can do nothing."

MIRIAM N. KOTZIN

ONLY

Today
the sea is gray
and cold. And the sky pale
as the old shirt you forgot when
you left.

The waves
rise and fall, just
as though they had nothing
else to do. Is that why I stand
watching?

Full moon.
A ghost crab comes
scuttling across the sand
and finds the plover chick asleep,
dinner.

SAFETY ZONE

We stayed to watch the full moon rise above
the distant palisades. We'd missed the last
full moon and more. We heard the mourning dove
whose soft and throaty call we thought we'd lost
when we moved here. We'd lost so much, at least
we still had that. Our foxgloves gone and all
the roses, and the mossy garden wall.

Almost the worst of all, we'd lost the sea.
We used to walk at dusk where spindrift blew,
and gulls stood by with stately courtesy
or, sullen, rose against the wind and flew
along the beach, First half the world was blue,
the sky and sea, and then it turned to pearl
a pink or gray. We'd watch the dusk unfurl.

The dusk was like a flag we'd fly to lift
our spirits, pipers chasing one last wave.
And still we spent those days with costly thrift.
If asked, we would have said that we'd been brave
for we had looked into the smallest grave,
together watched it close, as spade by spade
the earth … and hid the pine, the silk brocade.

MIRIAM N. KOTZIN

We left the foxgloves and the roses and
the mossy garden wall, and left behind
the gazing ball and fountain, the fairyland
that we had planned. Each week we'd find
our name, our places. We both waited, blind
as stone. And slowly sight returned. And night
was night. We moved. And I sat down to write.

PALMISTRY

I've heard that lifelines change.
If love lines also shift
and shorten, rearrange,
I've heard that lifelines change.
I do not think it strange
that fate can make lines drift.
I've heard that lifelines change
if love lines also shift.

MIRIAM N. KOTZIN

MIMOSA TREE

In summers past, that big, old tree
was covered with pink puffs that we
enjoyed together, for the bloom
would light our yard. We had no room
for sorrow then. And we felt free.

The flowers on its canopy
brought butterflies, a colony
of yellow flutter on perfume
in summers past.

Sometimes we sat and drank iced tea
and basked in our felicity.
We watched the iridescent zoom
of hummingbirds that fed on bloom
(our scarlet sage). We could agree
in summers past.

UNSPOKEN

I. He Says

Across the field the line of trees
stands dark against the winter sky
that's hanging low and gray. If I
guess right, it's snow tonight, an ease

into a subtle silence. These
are days we pause. We mollify.
Across the field the line of trees
stands dark against the winter sky.

It's just another sort of freeze;
we've come to know them both. I sigh
and bring in wood to keep it dry.
I can do that, I know, to please.
Across the field the line of trees
stands dark against the winter sky.

II. She Says

Perhaps because the dusk has come
upon us creeping down from gray
and heavy skies, I may betray
what's best concealed, my feeling numb.

MIRIAM N. KOTZIN

I'm almost sure that snow will come;
it's in the air. I've known all day.
Perhaps because the dusk has come,
I've nothing left I want to say.

I've work to do, and yet I drum
my fingers, waiting. Yesterday
the same. The room's in disarray.
How did our world slip out of plumb?
I've nothing left I want to say.

PATCH

Maybe because I watched her slink from
the neighbor's barn and stalk in waist-high
hay and over frozen stubble before I gave Patch

her name, or because I told him how she wound herself
around and around my legs, and how she appeared
like the night itself when the oblong of light spilled

from my window over the porch and came for milk
I poured in the white porcelain cup I'd slipped
from its hook for her, and how she'd allow just

the tips of my fingers in the soft thick scruff of her
fur as her pink tongue lapped up the warmed milk
and bump her head against my hand as I set down

the cup so she wore a splash of milk like a skullcap
while she drank, and how her breath hung in the icy air
like a useless wish, and how she stood with her forepaws

splayed, dark pads flattened against the glass,
her eyes green as winter moss on trees,
green as the evening sky before a summer storm,

green as the flash after the sun tumbles into the bay,
that's why just last Tuesday my husband gave Patch
to the gardener, who grinned and took her away.

MIRIAM N. KOTZIN

SPINDLES

We survive an insufficiency
of light. In pale rapidity
we grow to stalk and stem.
No flower, no fruit forms.
We fear our spindle kin.

For the sake of easy accounting,
say cruelty spindles our lives.
It spikes a shining running through
to keep us close by piercing.

THE PARTING

Today
the lane is lined
by a yellow riot,
forsythia, made wild by rain,
by wind.

I watched
you walk away
from me. You never looked
back. Your shoulders hunched, you kept your
head down.

Someone
who didn't know
would think you were cold or
looking for something precious you'd
just lost.

MIRIAM N. KOTZIN

Elevated Risks

ECHO

Surely these are my words,
and you have written them

before me. I recognize them
now, cool on white paper.

You speak to me shaken
from silence by my own voice.

MIRIAM N. KOTZIN

SECOND NATURE

He was right to be suspicious.
Even now I am conscious of betrayal.
But what did he expect when he dared

me to take his challenge? "Write a poem
using what I say. Quote me, Miriam, if
you can. Shape a world of your own

making. I'll stand in it laughing
at you the whole time. Why not
write about Edith Stein, a Jewish girl

who became a nun? They're working
on her sainthood now." Standing,
he looks cold. Yet his raincoat's never

buttoned, as though he's always on
his way to someplace warmer.
At the bar he seems almost at home.

"My father-in-law was a saint,"
the end's a certain martyrdom.
"His charity left no money." When

he talks about his daughters he names
only the younger, and her carefully.
His voice fills with love like a jug

with cool milk in summer. His
older daughter's gone, her name
changed willfully in a cloistered

order where all her art is given
over to God. Twice a year he
sees her through a grill. "I'm Jesuit

trained." He'd left the seminary.
Had his daughter meant to be
a son following a father's path, going

farther? How much patrimony? How
much vocation? How much unspoken love.
"Miriam," he says again, "write about
Edith Stein, the nun, my daughter."

TURN

after Whitman

I wear myself inside
out. If you miss

me, do not look now
under your boot soles.

I am not yet plotted.
I keep my heart still

where it belongs:
here in my mouth.

The Bachelor

All that the women left behind
were photos, records, bibelots, books.
Their trinkets filled the cozy nooks
of his condo and of his mind.

All his memorabilia lined
the walls, like shrunken heads on hooks.
All that the women left behind
were photos, records, bibelots, books.

With passing years he watched to find
which woman gave the closest looks.
He told them all they were so kind,
all the women left behind.

Miriam N. Kotzin

CHASE, TURN, DIP

Your name blinks on off on, bright
candy neon distraction light
flamingo night club pink, blaze blue
CIA to Noriega
rock I ride high, like a howdah,
waving to the crowds below. You

a lithe dancer, light on your feet,
change partners to a Latin beat,
chase, turn, dip, sweet moves I shimmy
down on, legs wrapped tight, and your name
shimmers, cha cha, mambo, it flames
sambas, your name lambadas me.

SWEAT RICE

After awhile, I understand
this Island-magic spell,
simple as boiling water.
Easy to become your
acquired taste: it just takes
rice, brown or white, cooked
as always in a heavy pot—
and my desire as I
squat naked over the rice,
thinking of you while the rising
steam trails insubstantial
plumes, warm as I know
your breath would be.
At first the steam is all
until, surrendering,
I grant you this knowledge:
molasses, salt, bitter melon.

MIRIAM N. KOTZIN

J'AI BAISÉ TA BOUCHE

After Salome by Aubrey Beardsley

Know. I would have taken
your breath
into my mouth like
honey sucked dripping

from the comb.

Your lips were still
soft beneath mine,
and when I bit you
did not flinch.

You do not turn
your face from me now,
Iokanaan,

though your
head grows heavy
in my hands.

J'ai baisé
ta bouche, Iokanaan.

Tell me.
If you could see
me now, Iokanaan,
how would you
ready yourself

for my kiss?

Miriam N. Kotzin

BUCK SEASON

This is the way we live:
we wake to news; flags
hang in ranks on screen.

We hear hunters' rifles.
Even at dawn we know
what counts. This windless

morning leaves do not
tremble, as though even
day holds its breath.

These woods are no
wilderness. Deer shelter
then come to our yard

to eat fallen apples as all
through the brazen summer
they claimed our garden.

They leap onto our roads.
We'll likely pass a fallen
deer, its long-lashed

eyes wide and blind, then
go on home, to sit, caught
by more grim news.

Elevated Risk

So now we do not choose to sit near trash
containers while we wait for trains. And if
we see a suitcase unattended, dash
to call police. Suspect each neckerchief.

We stand in crowded subways, and we sniff
for poison gas, which we've been told smells sweet
like new-mown grass, and hold our handkerchief
lest someone cough before we can retreat.

These days our outfit has to be complete
with compass, whistle, flashlight, knife—one must
have sturdy hiking boots. You are effete
without your hard hat. What for toxic dust?

I keep KI in case of dirty bomb—
I've extra cash. For now, I feel quite calm.

MIRIAM N. KOTZIN

STAY TUNED: MORE AT ELEVEN

She's sitting at the window looking out
into the street. She's watching cars go by,
some red, some blue. And when she hears a shout

she pays no mind. There's nothing strange about
those words she's heard so many times. And why
she's sitting at the window looking out

when they were driving by, guns drawn? Devout,
her grandma says, "God's will." The cars drive by,
some red, some blue. And when she hears a shout

the words are muffled by the glass. Without
more warning, come three aimless shots. No doubt
she's sitting at the window looking out

'cause nothing's on TV. "You fuck!" "Lookout!"
Those words she's heard too many times pass by,
some red, some blue. And when she hears a shout

it's all she hears, no shots. She's shot, snuffed out,
and soon official lights are flashing, fly—
some red, some blue—for when she hears the shout
she's sitting at the window looking out.

Virtual Siege

We've come to know the foreign war is far
from distant now. Dunes and palms are scenery
no more. In fact, the war is where we are.

The action's live, in time that's real. We're free
to turn it off or on, to turn away
from convoys, tanks, humvees, artillery.

So it's midnight here, there plus eight, it's day.
We watch the insubstantial columns rise
above the skyline: smoke that billows gray.

And here it's dusk, and there we see night skies
ablaze. The military experts trace
the course on maps, their faces lined and wise.

The breaking news is never commonplace:
we scan the screen to find just one loved face.

Miriam N. Kotzin

EUPHRATES

Perhaps the hanging gardens never did
exist. But "Babylon" can conjure still
an image of a high green weeping grid.

But now we hear the sirens' warning shrill
like some great mythic screeching bird, unseen
but for her shadow falling dark until

at last we see the night itself in green
through lenses that we use to trace the arc
of lines of fire across our TV screen.

We sit and listen to the sounds of stark
staccato bursts, fierce fusillades we know
as perforations of the silent dark.

How tall the reeds along the river grow
where one small white bird fell not long ago.

Winter Bloom

On Thirteenth Street I find some trees
in bloom. I make a mental note:
return, return. Why don't they freeze?
The answer's underground, remote
uninsulated pipes. I gloat

at having found these blossoms now,
for all the other trees are bare,
and these, anomalies, allow
a moment to reflect. Aware
my spring's in doubt, I stop to stare

at these reminders scattered pink
along dark winter-barren boughs.
They're pale, and open wide. I think
about the spring ahead, my vows
to make each day suffice. The plows

have passed. They cleared the street of snow.
And somewhere underground there's heat
that I can't feel. And yet I know
that it might coax or force a fleet-
ing bloom, unseasonably sweet.

MIRIAM N. KOTZIN

In Centralia

For more than forty years the fire
has been burning. I know where
and how it smolders and flares.

I have mapped its progress
in darkness, but such knowledge
gives no dominion over burning.

I am accustomed to danger,
to the curiosity of strangers.

Attempts to starve the fire
only stoke the flames
threatening to consume me.

How the burning started is
irrelevant. Ask why I choose
to stay here, in Centralia.

Weights & Measures

Autumn Sunset with Starlings

For weeks we watched the sugar maples flare
along our street. At first it was a slow
but certain simmer going golden there

up high where most sun struck the tree: a glow
at first, mere hint, until at last the green
gave way to yellow, orange, red. A flow

of color blazed. And in the blaze unseen,
a flock of starlings perched among the leaves
and twittered, tuneless, hidden by the screen

of flames. Then something sudden startles, heaves
into the air, a dark net, starlings fly,
each bird a knot, the flock in flight unweaves.

The net is cast, attenuates, flung high,
Then gathers, sinks and settles like a sigh.

Miriam N. Kotzin

MORNING OFFICE

This morning when I woke, the woods were gone,
for they'd dissolved in fog, as though the snow
that lay upon the ground had wished to go
back up; a cloud had settled on the lawn
to carry off the snow. Oblivion
must be like this, I thought, and then a crow
came through the fog, an omen neatly drawn.

At dawn the world was wholly silent; stilled
the birds whose morning songs I loved, and then
the silence seeped indoors, an eerie hush
that filled my room as though the fog had spilled
within. One cry the only sound: again
the crow came flying from the underbrush.

NOVEMBER SNOW

The slow snow fills the dark
crotch of the maple and lights
on limbs. It draws us up
to an extenuating calligraphy
of twigs, of a distant blush,
of a deep spell that holds
until its cryptic green unfolds.

MIRIAM N. KOTZIN

PALETTE

Although we think of spring as being green
and gold, a bloom of white and pink, I've found
it's not.   It's really something in between

bright blossoms and new leaves and winter's mien.
Unplowed, the stubbled fields of corn abound,
although we think of spring as being green.

The milkweed pods are open beaks I've seen
on baby birds, the ragged silk, their sound.
Or not. It's really something in between

such squawks and song like silk chiffon. Routine
surveyance of the season will confound.
Although we think of spring as being green,

the trees in distant woods are red, a screen
of russet lace aloft. Their green's renowned.
They're not. They're really something in between

one palette and another, both serene.
This single season is a middle ground.
Although we think of spring as being green,
t's not. It's really something in between.

WHIMSIES

On the bushes down the lane
droplets hang after a long rain.
Last fall red berries
hung where now hang there
clear whimsies
on each cane.

MIRIAM N. KOTZIN

INVENTORY

After Frost

The light is golden at this time of day.
As afternoon subsides, in this slow spill
as thick as syrup, cloying sweet, the field
is glazed with gold. Today it's warm. They say
tomorrow it will snow. This is the way
that spring comes in. Now gold, then snow's white will
prevails in spring's first days. We've learned to yield
to each dawn's pale surprise of light or snow.
The pear will soon be trimmed with snow. Come May,
it will be white again with bloom. We fill
our lives with what we have, what is. Annealed
by loss, we can endure. All slips away.
Just now the field is sweetened, glazed with gold:
we learn to treasure what we cannot hold.

FLAME AZALEAS

Along the road are woods where wild
azaleas grow. Their orange flames
the wood, and, passing, we're beguiled.
These woods are blazing, bright with fire.
Spring pools are gone to flame, have burned;
they flame untouched by our desire.

MIRIAM N. KOTZIN

PRESCIENCE

Before the dusk arrives, before the shift
of light, the tallest trees begin to mark
the change of day as lightly breezes lift.

On trembling leaves the sun ignites a spark
that leaps from branch to swaying branch, and then
insistent rustling—hours yet till dark.

And all the leaves grow wild with wind, and when
the shadow creeps across the field it seems
the frantic leaves refuse to hush again.

And then they're still. And dusk. And smallest gleams
now slowly rise in nets of light that drift
up through the night like half-remembered dreams.

These float through dawn and into day. This gift
suggests all needs, provides a borrowed thrift.

Night Lake

Before us lay the lake all shining black
and gold. The full moon spilled a path of light.
We heard a splash: a frog or fish had leapt
into the air and fallen back. What were
we thinking when we chose to come to this
deserted place? We nudge the boat away
from shore; we slice through water and we move
out on the lake. We head straight for the moon,
and glide on guided by a distant hoot.
We know that in a full-leaved tree an owl
is perched and somewhere on the forest floor
in fallen leaves a mouse or chipmunk waits.
The owl sends soft and softer calls, to ask
the only question now: *whose death, whose death?*

Miriam N. Kotzin

OPEN SECRET

The oak leaves glisten in the sun. I hear
the adumbrations of the wind that warn
of coming winter in the hushing leaves.

I stop to listen to the wind in sere
brown leaves. I know the language. It's inborn.
I know to halt, attend the falling leaves.

The oak leaves glisten. In the sun I hear
the mockingbirds' glib repertoire. I scorn
the borrowed sequenced liquid songs of thieves.

I stop to listen. To the wind in sere
brown leaves the grasses whisper back the sworn
but open secret telling why man grieves.

The wind slips through the needles of the pine
whose wood's the bed where I will last recline.

PERPETUAL CARE

Each time I go I wonder what I'll find,
perhaps some weeds, perhaps a tilted stone;
the tilted headstone must be realigned.

How did the granite footstone chip? The tone
I have to take when I complain must be
polite without my seeming to condone.

I see another nearby grave's been filled,
or should I say it has been occupied—
A working backhoe suddenly is stilled.

I worry that the fresh dug grave beside
my father's has encroached into his space;
I speak to both before I turn aside.

But at my last arrival at this place
I will be missing neither voice nor face.

MIRIAM N. KOTZIN

Like This

for Moshe Meyer Etkin

The numbers on the walk were worn away
by steps and time so what the office gave
me proved of little help to find his grave.
I took my time. I'd lots of time that day
to look. I knew that it was on the right
according to the card the office kept.
I counted rows, was careful as I stepped.
A sunny day, the stones were washed with light.

Because no paths were made between the rows
of stones, I walked and stood on graves. I bent
to read the names the marble markers held
a hundred years to find one to disclose
that here my father's mother's father went
whose name, on rain-worn stone, these fingers spelled.

LIMINAL

This is the place my father, dying, chose
to lie. His parents, here, grandparents, too,
an aunt, a brother. Surely he'd propose
we gather here. And what were we to do?

We'd acquiesce, of course. For why review
the pros and cons of place? It was foregone
we'd go along, then go along. We knew
we'd land here, crammed together in a lawn.

I know I'll be the last to see the view,
for I can see no body follows me.
I look ahead and finding there no queue
descending, fault my fruitless husbandry.

And when, at last, to this place I've been sent,
Earth, be both caul and best integument.

MIRIAM N. KOTZIN

DECEMBER 12, 1983

That long December day
she lay
alone, no longer ill,
so, still
without a hand to hold,
so, cold
in that blue light, I told
her one last secret: Why.
I didn't want to cry.
She lay so still, so cold.

COSSACK

Death, you have become so clever.
While I watched, you bagged my father,
mother, but left me
alone—to bury
them, to be their mourner.

I used to imagine you all
got up as a young Cossack, tall
on his horse, openly
vicious. I could see
your face, glee-lit. Recall

how you rode in with polished black
boots, sword bright, flashing, to attack.
The setting sun stained
your horse's flanks, veined,
straining, reined. The sharp crack

of your coming. The dried mud dark
on your mount's legs, and one thin mark
on your sleeve revealed
where you'd been afield.
Oh, I steeled myself. Stark

against this white page, you can still
disappear, vanish, when you will.
Though you never leave,
yet I can't conceive
you, but grieve the lost thrill

MIRIAM N. KOTZIN

of the sound of your swift coming.
No, now you are so small, the ring
on my finger slips
over you. My lips
lisp courtship's opening.

When you came, I heard instead
of thundering hooves, or boots tread,
when you came into
me, I heard the dew
rise. I knew what you'd said,

whose insinuations are no
metaphors. Blood borne, you grow
familiar as the beat
of my pulse, the heat
of the sweet fever, slow.

Death, you have grown too small for
your own boots, Oh, my conqueror,
I encompass you
entirely. Do
you see? You die in me.

PAROLE

I hear the distant somber call
from down in the woods at nightfall,
resonant and deep
reminder that sleep
in earth's keep
comes to all.

Sleep's a meek evasion. It's death
in the owl's call and the wind's low breath.
The evening's clear.
The nocturnal air
that I hear
is the scythe.

GOING UNDER

I. Tonsillectomy

The first time I went under I was four,
a simple tonsillectomy. She lied
and promised I'd smell oranges. She wore
a mask, had smiling eyes. I'm told I cried.

I watched while she took something bad and held
it on my face. And that was all. I woke
up in a room with mom and dad. "It smelled,"
I said. But now my throat hurt when I spoke.

I still feel cheated of that promised smell
of orange. And even now I wonder why
I should remember that detail and dwell
upon it. Wasn't it a harmless lie?

I'm sure they all meant only to be kind
to me, yet I can guess just why I mind.

II: Partial Oophorectomy

And when the stakes were higher at the next
occasion I lay waiting, stashed, on drip,
for hours in a basement hall: a text-
book case of cysts. I never thought to rip

the tube out from my arm and run, a tip
I might have taken had I known. I lay
apart from all the lively fellowship
that flowed in eddies down the hall. The day

began: a gurney ride, a passageway,
and I'd been shaved and warned the night before.
The left and right were both involved, no way
to tell just what would be. They'd cut, explore.

They told me that the cysts were all benign;
they never promised, gutted, I'd be fine.

III. Discectomy

It came to this: I had no choice unless
a sure paralysis was fine with me.
The risk reward was easy to assess—
mere ten percent against a certainty.
And so, I found it easy to say yes
and sign the legal forms. My strategy
just now is to omit, no, to compress
the pain and loss that led to surgery.

In case you care: I walk, I feel, maintain
control of functions I won't name. That night
I had the surgery, they showed me how

to kneel, my knees apart. On drip, both pain
and modesty were gone. I got it right,
and lay like jam on evening sky somehow.

IV. Perimenopausal Dilation and Curettage

I'm sure this should have been a piece of cake;
for at this point I'd nothing much to lose,
or so they said. But that depends on who's
the judge, and who decides just what's at stake.
I'd heard it said there's nothing much about
a D&C to cause alarm. And as
the doctor said, it's wait and see. He has
an eager resident to scrape, no doubt.

I'd nothing more to do. I just lay back
to wait until the anesthesia hit.
And then I got a swell idea: I'd fight
to stay awake. Around the cul-de-sac
and round I'd go, not spinning out, one... bit.
And I was gone. So was the doctor right?

V. Colonoscopy

One likes to say the prep's the hardest part
of this procedure. One could say it's not
the prep that's bad at all. The prep's an art,

a masterful distraction that's designed
to keep one focused on detail, a smart
magician's waving hand, a trick refined

so one is fooled—it's like the waving cape
the matador will shake and swirl. One's blind,
forgets why one has come. One can escape.

And like the bull, one can be sweet-talked by
a murmured, "toro, toro," miss the scrape
of spade that gravely warns, "You, too, will die."

And that's the hardest part: not how, nor why.
We won't hear scrape, or thud, or rope's long sigh.

MIRIAM N. KOTZIN

APPETITE

She takes her place in line content to wait
her turn to reach the food that sits on shelves
in tidy rows: the cardboard pies, each plate
aligned, the cottage cheese and pears that elves
arranged near squares of cake. Deliberate
as though it matters, jelled desserts, by twelves
that glow, suspend bright fruit to celebrate
imagined joys of those who help themselves.

She chooses tasteless food and fills her tray
with plastic plates. The cubes of green and red
all quiver as she slides it down to pay.
She waits for change, remembers what was said
about the scan. The doctor's voice was gray
as steel, as though he also dared not feel.

REMISSION

I hold the mango in my palm.
I push the knife through the skin,
incise, knife point tracing oval seed.

I remember the summer we ate
cold soup of ripe mango,
raw sweet corn, and jalapeños.

The knife might slip, for
my fingers are slick with
the juice of ripe mango.

I hold the last mango in my palm;
it is the weight of one breast.
That summer we ate cold soup.

MIRIAM N. KOTZIN

PORTRAIT

When she smiles, it is like light
wind lifting the leaves
of the yellow quaking aspen

that stands like a sentinel
at the far corner of the yard
keeping uneasy watch.

Her eyes suggest the light
admonishment of morning
caught on a filmed pane.

She lies on the sofa like light
of late winter afternoons
when curtains are pulled back

by one standing at a window
as if to watch the last of day
or to welcome night.

My Landscape

The ochre grasses rise above
the snowy field. A mourning dove
is crooning songs of muted love.
My winter landscape is not grim.

The forest bordering the field
seems almost lavender, revealed
through fog. This is winter's yield.
My winter landscape is not grim.

The branches of the sycamore
are ghostly bare. A wild corps
of black birds, startled, call and soar.
My winter landscape is not grim.

By looking out I've come to terms
I can't negotiate. The berms
I crawl on lead at last to worms.
No winter landscape is not grim.

Miriam N. Kotzin

CALENDAR

In spring, when all the blooming world seems young
and I feel young no more, I'm not downcast.
Instead I bide my time and hold my tongue,
for winter's cold will come to all at last.

Then follows summer's heat when life is bright,
and all the pretty little blooms are massed.
I know it only seems to be all right,
for winter's cold will come to all at last.

Next follows full-leaved fall, that's really cool;
This brightest season comes and goes too fast,
so I just watch the others play the fool,
for winter's cold will come to all at last.

And then the winter comes. The skies grow gray
when all the cloudless blues of fall have passed
and all the golds and reds have blown away:
for winter's cold will come to all at last.

This coldest season's seasoned with a twist,
of which I'm now a true enthusiast.
At last I'm forced to be an optimist
to keep the winter's cold from me at last.

Weights and Measures

Where once red berries
grew now hang drops
of rain. Dry sepals
hold these which feed
no bird but wind.

In each a world
depends, inverse,
in small.

Miriam N. Kotzin

INTERIOR DESIGN

How long ago and why did winter tear
apart last summer's wasps' gray paper nest,
the paper nest, now torn past all repair?

What we see now exposed was always there:
while whole, remained invisible, unguessed.
How long ago and why did winter tear

the flowing paper waves? We find a rare
collector's print—we see where those waves crest—
the paper nest, now torn past all repair.

This empty paper nest was built with care
or instinct. I don't know, nor have I guessed
how long ago. And why did winter tear

it down? Has winter built it new? See where
the wild sea's held still in paper, pressed.
The paper nest, now torn past all repair!

The wasps are gone, so I can stand and stare
at all that they and time have made, have blessed.
How long ago and why did winter tear
the paper nest, now torn past all repair?

ANYWAY

I saw a flying wasp just yesterday
near last year's ruined nest. All torn apart
it cleaves: exposed gray tattered paper heart.

I'm sure it must be empty now. It lay
like some cross-sectioned bio textbook art.
I saw a flying wasp just yesterday
near last year's ruined nest, all torn apart.

It hovered near the nest. I cannot say
if thought or instinct brought it there to start
another summer's day—or to impart
a Providential lesson. Anyway,
I saw a flying wasp just yesterday.

MIRIAM N. KOTZIN

LEAVES

When the first leaf fell,
it did not ride the wind,
but drifted, in a slow spin
from limb to ground. Now
leaves dip and swoop,
waltzing like finches.
Dry oak leaves scatter
light like spilled glitter.
Leaves tick against the
window. All around
us, light and flutter.
Along the woodland path,
a few final flowers:
here, fall's violet aster
and the last of summer's
pale gold touch-me-not,
jewel weed—and there, light
yellow swamp candle
and pink lady's thumb—and
there, white snakeroot.
I fumble, wanting to give you
their names, anything,
to remember.

Acknowledgments

"Anyway" [appeared as "Euphoriant"], *Front Street Review*, Spring 2004; "Autumn Landscape with Starlings," *Boulevard*, Fall 2008; "Back" [appeared as "Beach House"], *Alehouse Review*, Fall, 2006; "Buck Season," *Vocabula Review*, December 2005; "Cossack," *Southern Hum*, December 2005; "Elevated Risk," *Vocabula Review*, December 2005 (*Vocabula, Bound II,* 2008) and *Gator Springs Gazette*, September/October 2004; "Euphrates," *Front Street Review*, Spring 2004; "Ghost Crabs," *Southern Hum*, December 2005; "Going Under," *Drexel Online Journal*, August 2004; "Impressionism on the Beach," *Southern Hum*, December 2005; "J'ai Baisé ta Bouche," *Salomé*, Monday, March 7, 2005; "Laundry" [appeared as "Homemaker's Rondeau"], *Another Toronto Quarterly*, July 2004; "Leaves," *Carnelian*, July 2004; "Like This," *Boulevard*, Spring 2006; "Liminal," *Segue*, November 2004; "Morning Office," *Vocabula Review*, December 2005; "My Landscape," in *Vocabula Review*, March 2004; "Open Secret," *Boulevard*, Fall 2008; "Palette," *Eclectica*, July/August 2004; "Perpetual Care," *Boulevard*, Spring 2006; "Safety Zone," *Southern Hum*, December 2005; "Second Nature," *FRiGG*, January 2005; "Sweat Rice," *Poems Niederngasse*, erotic supplement, February 2006; "The Bachelor," *Era*, Vol. 12, Spring 1977; "Turn," *Mickle Street Review*, Fall 2004: "Virtual Siege," *Maverick Magazine*, July 4, 2004; "Unspoken" [appeared as "Unspoken Dialogue"], *Carnelian*, 2005:"Weights and Measures," *Boulevard*, Spring 2006; "Whimsies," BLAST, December 20, 2005.

MIRIAM N. KOTZIN, associate professor of English at Drexel University, directs the Certificate Program in Writing and Publishing and teaches creative writing and literature. Her fiction and poetry have been published widely in literary journals. She is a contributing editor of *Boulevard* and a founding editor of *Per Contra: the International Journal of the Arts, Literature and Ideas.* She is the author of *A History of Drexel University* (Drexel University, 1983) and two collections of poetry, *Reclaiming the Dead* (New American Press, 2008) and *Weights & Measures* (Star Cloud Press, 2009).

Printed in the United States
222292BV00001B/1/P